FAMOUS RUSSIAN RECIPES

FAMOUS RUSSIAN RECIPES

TRANSLATED by SASHA KASHEVAROFF
THIRD EDITION
REVISED by MARGARET CALVIN
ILLUSTRATIONS by SANDY GRIFFITH

OLD HARBOR PRESS
SITKA • ALASKA

First Edition 1936
Second Edition copyright 1969 by Sitka Printing Co.
Third Edition copyright 1985 by Old Harbor Press
Second Printing 1988
Third Printing 1993
International Standard Book Number: 0-9615529-2-1
Printed in the United States of America
All rights reserved

OLD HARBOR PRESS
Publishers and Printers
P.O. BOX 97 SITKA, ALASKA 99835

Contents

Introduction 7
Translator's Note 9

LUNCH and SUPPER DISHES
Salmon Pie
   Pirog iz Sjomgii 13
Salmon Filets
   Sjomga 14
Chicken Aspic
   Kooriza Zaleevnoie 15
Roasted Wild Duck
   Zarenaja Dikaja Ootka 16
Cabbage (Sauté - Hash - Pie)
   Kapoosta 17
Mushroom Patties
   Gribamii Piroshki 18
Stuffed Noodles in Bouillon
   Pelmenee 19
Pre-Lenten Pancakes
   Bleenee 20
Beet Soup
   Borsch 21

DESSERTS
Apple or Plum Tort
   Jablochnii Slibovii Tort 25
Apple Roll
   Struscheli 26
Easter Pudding
   Paskha 27

Contents

DESSERTS Continued
   Pastry with Strawberry Jam and Whipped Cream
      Piroznoie s Malinoii i Sbitimii Slivkamii 28
   Rice-Orange Pudding
      Apelsinovii Pooding 29

BREADS and SMALL PASTRIES
   Easter Bread
      Kulich 33
   Braided Roll
      Pletjonaja Boolka 34
   Cottage Cheese Tarts
      Vatrooshki 35
   Cracknels
      Suharji 36
   Carrot-Egg Turnover
      Piroshki 37

MISCELLANEOUS
   Russian Tea
      Russkii Chai 41
   Salt Herring Appetizer
      Zakooska Selyodka 42
   Mustard Sauce
      Garchichij Sous 43

INTRODUCTION

Alaska has a strong Russian tradition. This is particularly true of Sitka, in southeast Alaska, which served as the capital of Russian America for many years, and was the site of the transfer of Alaska to the United States in 1867. After the transfer many Russian families elected to remain in Sitka, thus perpetuating Russian names, customs--and foods.

This small cookbook is an effort to save some of the better known recipes that were used in those Russian households, and subsequently by other Sitkans who may have had their first glimpse of a Kulich at a bake sale held by the women of the Russian Church.

Physically this church, St. Michael's Cathedral, dominates the Sitka landscape, being situated in the middle of the main street with traffic flowing on either side. Culturally, the church's presence is also felt. Its bells ring for services and the active congregation still has a procession around the building on Easter Eve. Sitka celebrates two Christmases and two Easters, each first by the Gregorian calendar followed about two weeks later by the Russian celebration using the Julian calendar. Sitka accommodates both by putting up Christmas decorations after Thanksgiving and leaving them up until after Russian New Year.

Often the Russian customs and events are celebrated with food, particularly at Easter which probably surpasses Christmas in importance in the Russian household. The Easter table is spread with an assortment of main dishes, pastries and puddings, all of which have been carefully prepared to exhibit the skills of the cook.

Sasha Kashevaroff was raised in this Russian tradition. Her father was a Russian priest and so she knew well the fasting of Lent, the joy of Easter, the beauty of Christmas. She was born in Kodiak but the family moved to various West Coast locations, including Sitka, where she returned to stay in the early 1930's as a young adult. Well known for her cooking, she introduced her guests to many of the foods presented here. This, combined with her wit and easy manner of entertaining, have left fond memories of evenings at her home.

Interest in Sitka's Russian background is catching to many newcomers and Sandy Griffith is one who has been caught up in it. Born and raised in Plainview, Texas, Sandy came to Sitka in 1979 and soon started studying the traditional Russian designs. Through her artwork she makes it possible for each of us to have a glimpse of Russian Sitka and to feel the richness and fun of that heritage.

This book is essentially a product of Sitka, which has been home to its translator, artist and reviser and is the place of its publication. The first two editions and the first printing of the third edition were printed by *letterpress* from hand set type on a platen press and bound in Sitka. Subsequent printings have been by *photo-offset* using the *letterpress* text for copy.

In revising this little cookbook, my aim has been similar to Sasha's back in 1936 for the first edition: to adapt the recipes to use ingredients, equipment and methods currently available without losing the flavor of the end product or the charm of the original translation.

I would like to dedicate this edition to my late husband, Jack Calvin, who was my mentor in this business and so started the printer's ink flowing in my veins. And I would like to thank all the friends and relatives who helped in so many ways, including testing the recipes and giving comments and suggestions. Thanks to Sandy Griffith who encouraged me to continue the project when I suddenly became not only reviser, but also printer and publisher. And a special thanks to Natasha Calvin (Jack and Sasha's daughter), Bob Ellis, Carolyn Servid, and Mary Clay Muller for their invaluable assistance in editing and proofreading.

MARGARET CALVIN

Sitka, Alaska
1988

Translator's Note

The recipes in this book have been selected from hundreds in a Russian cookbook called *A Present for Young Housewives*, by E. Molokhovetz. Their choice has been dictated by a desire to introduce to American housewives some of the famous and characteristic dishes that made cooking a fine art in Sitka, as well as in old Russia. Thanks to modern methods of stocking our kitchen shelves, the preparation of these dishes is now less of an art (and less of an ordeal) than in the days when the Double Eagle flew over the Castle [in Sitka]. Buying a yeast cake, for example, is a simpler process than tenderly nursing a batch of home-made yeast. Hence it has been possible to simplify most of these recipes in translation, often reducing a day's work to an hour's, and bringing once complicated dishes well within the scope of the present-day housewife's kitchenette and temperament. The simplification entails no loss of quality, however. Indeed, the contrary is likely to be true, and the housewife who tries out on her family one of the simpler dishes, such as Borsch, may find that she has created a lively demand not only for more Borsch, but for Bleenee, Pirog, Kulich, etc.

SASHA KASHEVAROFF

Sitka, Alaska
1936

St. Michael's Cathedral
Sitka, Alaska

LUNCH
and
SUPPER DISHES

Pirog iz Sjomgii

SALMON PIE

Puff paste:
- 1 cup shortening
- 2½ cups flour
- ⅓ tsp. salt
- water (about ½ cup)

Cut shortening into sifted flour and salt. Add only enough water to hold pastry together; mix lightly; transfer to a floured board. Using about two-thirds of the dough, roll it out and fit into the bottom and sides of an 8 x 8 x 2 inch pan.

Filling:
- ¾ cup rice
- ½ tsp. salt
- 1½ cups water
- 2 cups sliced onion
- 2 cups sliced cabbage (optional)
- 1 tbsp. shortening
- 1 lb. salmon, fresh or canned
- 2 hard boiled eggs, chopped
- salt and pepper to taste
- butter

Cook rice with salt in water over low heat until water is absorbed and rice is tender. Fry onion and cabbage in shortening with salt and pepper until lightly browned. If fresh salmon is used, filet it (page 14).

Put half the rice on the crust. Lay fish on rice; season with salt and pepper. Distribute the onions and cabbage; then the chopped eggs; and finally the remaining rice. Dot with butter. Cover with remaining dough. Slit top crust well to permit steam to escape. If using fresh salmon, bake 1 hour in a moderate oven (350°F). If canned salmon is used, reduce baking time to one-half hour in a very hot oven (450°F). Serve with mayonnaise-cheese sauce (page 14). Pirog may be frozen either before or after baking.

Yield: 6 servings.

Sjomga

SALMON FILETS

2 lb. fresh salmon, cut in 1 piece
salt and pepper to taste
2 tbsp. flour
4 tbsp. shortening or oil
2 tbsp. mayonnaise
½ cup cream
½ cup grated cheddar cheese

With a sharp knife filet fish by cutting in half along backbone and slipping knife carefully between ribs and flesh, thus removing all bone. With the pieces lying skin-side down on a board, cut the fish off the skin. Then cut into pieces about 2 x 3 inches. Season with salt and pepper and roll in flour. Fry gently in hot oil being careful not to overcook.

Serve with cheese sauce made by gently warming mayonnaise, cream and cheese in double boiler until cheese melts.

Yield: 4 servings.

The importance of cutting fish as described above cannot be over emphasized. Fish so cut retains moisture and flavor that are lost if the fish is cut in the more conventional across-the-back-bone steaks.

Kooriza Zaleevnoie

CHICKEN ASPIC

1 2½ to 3 lb. chicken
⅔ cup sliced carrot
¾ cup sliced onion

1 tsp. salt	½ cup water
⅛ tsp. pepper	1 egg, hard boiled
2 tbsp. vinegar	1 pickled beet
1 tbsp. gelatine	1 tbsp. capers

1 small jar stuffed olives

Cut the chicken into pieces and cover with cold water (about 4 cups). Add carrot, onion, salt and pepper and bring to a boil. When chicken is tender, strain and cool the bouillon. Remove fat from the bouillon, add vinegar and bring to a boil. Soften gelatine in water. Pour 2 cups of the boiling bouillon over the gelatine. Set aside to cool. Remove meat from the bones and cut into small pieces. Slice hard boiled egg, pickled beet and olives.

When bouillon has cooled, pour a half cup into a large mold or 8 x 8 inch cake pan. When it is set, arrange slices of egg, beet, capers and olives on the jelly. Carefully pour on more of the bouillon. When this has set until it is fairly stiff, distribute the chicken over the jelly and pour on the remaining bouillon.

When ready to serve, remove from mold onto platter, garnish with lettuce, etc., and serve with mayonnaise or mustard sauce (page 43).

Yield: 6 to 8 servings.

Zarenaja Dikaja Ootka

ROASTED WILD DUCK

Clean and wash the duck. Put chopped apple inside (never stuff a wild duck) and put into greased roasting pan. Pop the duck into a very hot oven (500°F) and roast for exactly one-half hour, basting with the drippings every five minutes Serve immediately.

If you like your duck well done, preheat the oven to 450°F. Place the bird in the oven and reduce heat immediately to 325°F. Cook until tender allowing about 30 minutes per pound.

Yield: 2 servings.

Kapoosta

CABBAGE

Basic Cabbage Sauté

- 4 cups thinly sliced or shredded cabbage
- 1½ cups thinly sliced onion
- 3 tbsp. butter or margerine
- salt and pepper to taste
- 1 tbsp. water

Fry cabbage and onion in butter or margerine with salt and pepper over low heat until lightly brown Add water, cover and cook for 1 minute.

Yield: 4 one-half cup servings.

Cabbage Hash

Add to basic recipe and cook until thoroughly warm:

- 2 cups ground or chopped cooked roast beef or other meat
- 2 tbsp. butter or margerine

Yield: 6 servings.

Cabbage Pie

Make pastry to line an 8 x 8 x 2 inch pan and for a top crust (page 13). Fill with cabbage hash. Bake in a hot oven (500°F) for about 15 minutes or until lightly brown. Serve with sour cream or gravy. This is a favorite Russian dish.

Yield: 6 servings.

Gribamii Piroshki

MUSHROOM PATTIES

Patty Shells: (Small toast squares may be substituted.)
- 1 cup flour
- ⅓ cup shortening
- ¼ tsp. salt
- water

Filling:
- 2 cups diced onion
- 1 tbsp. butter
- ½ lb. mushrooms, sliced
- 1 tbsp. flour
- 1 cup milk
- salt and pepper to taste

Patty shells: Using only enough water to bind, make a pastry of the flour, shortening and salt. Roll out to an eighth inch thick and cut into 3 to 4 inch rounds. Line muffin tins with the rounds by fitting the pastry loosely into the pan and pressing it firmly around the sides. Prick with a fork and bake in a hot oven (425°F) for 10 to 12 minutes or until light brown.

Filling: Fry onion gently in butter until clear. Add mushrooms and cook 5 minutes. Sprinkle with flour and stir. Add milk, salt and pepper and cook over low heat until thick, stirring often. Pour into the patty shells or over toast squares.

Yield: 15 to 20 patties.

Pelmenee

STUFFED NOODLES IN BOUILLON

Stuffing:
 ½ cup chopped onion ⅓ lb. ground lean beef
 ¼ tbsp. butter ⅓ lb. ground lamb or
 salt and pepper to taste pork

Noodles:
 2 cups flour 1 whole egg
 ½ tsp. salt 2 egg yolks
   ¼ cup water

Bouillon:
 2½ quarts beef bouillon made from:
  10 beef bouillon cubes dissolved in 10 cups water
  or
  4 10½ oz. cans beef consommé diluted with 5 cups water

Fry onion in butter until light brown. Add to uncooked meats, season to taste, mix well and set aside.

Make a stiff dough of the flour, salt, egg, egg yolks and water. Knead well and divide into four approximately equal parts. Taking one part at a time, roll out on floured board as thin as possible without breaking (about 16 inch diameter) and cut into rounds with a 2 inch biscuit cutter.

Put about a half teaspoon stuffing on one half of each round of dough. Moisten edges with water, fold over, making half rounds, and seal edges with a fork. Then bring together the points of the half rounds, pinching to make cap-shaped forms.

Divide the bouillon into two kettles and bring to a boil. Drop one-quarter of the caps into the boiling bouillon in each kettle and boil 15 minutes. A few are cooked at a time to avoid cooling the bouillon. Serve immediately in bouillon in large soup plates.

Yield: 8 to 10 servings.

Bleenee

PRE-LENTEN PANCAKES

1½ tsp. dry yeast	2 tsp. melted butter
or ½ yeast cake	1 tsp. salt
3 cups warm milk	1 egg yolk
1¼ cups white flour	1 cup buckwheat flour
1 tsp. sugar	1 egg white, well beaten
⅓ cup thick cream	

Soften yeast in one-half cup of warm milk. Into remaining milk slowly stir the white flour, sugar and melted butter. Add yeast. Beat until smooth and put in warm place until well raised (about one and one-half hours). When raised, beat in the salt and egg yolk. Add the buckwheat flour and beat well. Carefully stir in the beaten egg white and cream. Raise again. Then, without stirring again, cook like pancakes, using a 7 or 8 inch frying pan. Make each cake the full size of the pan.

Yield: 12 to 15 pancakes.

Just before the lean days of Lent rich foods are in order and fluffy Bleenee, liberally buttered and eaten with caviar or pickled herring, is a favorite supper dish. They are also good at breakfast with fried apples, rhubarb or other cooked fruit, or for supper with fish baked in a sauce.

Borsch

BEET SOUP

2 medium size beets
4 cups beef bouillon made from:
  2 10½ oz. cans beef consommé
  diluted with 1½ cups water
  or
  4 beef bouillon cubes dissolved
  in 4 cups water
1 cup chopped carrot
1 cup chopped onion
1 bayleaf (optional)
⅓ cup diced ham or fried bacon bits
½ cup tomato juice
1½ cups chopped cabbage
½ cup sour cream
croutons (optional)

In a saucepan boil beets with enough water to cover until tender (from one-half to one hour depending on freshness). Skin them while still warm.

In another saucepan combine beef bouillon with carrot, onion and bayleaf. Boil half an hour.

Cube the beets and add to bouillon along with the ham or bacon, tomato juice and cabbage. Boil until the cabbage is done. When serving add a generous tablespoon of sour cream to each dish and garnish with croutons.

Yield: 4 one and one-half cup servings.

Few are the first rate cooks in any land who will not smile at the word "borsch," for of all Russian dishes it is the best known—and there are probably as many ways of making it as there are Russian cooks.

Double-Headed Eagle
Russian Imperial Emblem

DESSERTS

Jablochnii Slibovii Tort

APPLE or PLUM TORT

1 cup butter	2 eggs, beaten
½ cup sugar	4 tsp. sugar
2½ cups flour	Plum jam or thick,
½ tsp. salt	sweet applesauce

Cream butter and one-half cup sugar. Add flour and salt. Set aside about one-quarter of the beaten eggs and add remaining eggs to the dough. Spread into two 9 inch cake pans. Spread the reserved egg over the two parts and sprinkle with 4 tsp. sugar. Bake in a medium oven (350°F) about 30 minutes.

Remove from pans. Place one layer on a serving platter and spread with jam or applesauce. Cover with second layer and spread more jam or applesauce on top. Serve sliced, either hot or cold.

Yield: 10 to 12 servings.

Struscheli

APPLE ROLL

Pastry:
 1¾ cups flour
 2¼ tsp. baking powder
 ¼ cup sugar
 ½ tsp. salt
 ¼ cup butter
 2 eggs, beaten
 ⅓ cup cream
 2 tbsp. soft butter

Filling:
 3 cups chopped tart apples
 ¾ cup seedless raisins, steamed until soft
 2 tbsp. sugar
 ⅛ tsp. cinnamon

Topping:
 1 tbsp. sugar
 1 tsp. cinnamon

Pastry: Sift together the flour, baking powder, sugar and salt. Cut one-fourth cup butter into these ingredients using a pastry blender or two knives. Add cream to eggs and beat. Make a well in the dry ingredients and pour the liquid into it. Combine with a few swift strokes. Handle the dough as little as possible. On floured wax paper, roll out to about a 10 inch square. Spread with soft butter.

Filling: Mix ingredients and spread on dough. Roll up by using the wax paper to support the dough, removing the paper as the roll forms. Transfer roll to baking sheet.

Topping: Mix ingredients and sprinkle on top of roll.

Roll may be either baked in one piece or cut before baking like cinnamon rolls. Bake in a moderate oven (350°F) for 30 minutes.

Yield: 6 to 8 servings.

Paskha

EASTER PUDDING

2 lb. dry or large curd cottage cheese	1 cup sugar
½ cup butter	⅔ cup whipping cream
4 egg yolks	½ cup raisins, steamed
	¼ cup almonds, cut fine

Also needed are cheesecloth and a mold such as a flower pot, tofu press or other arrangement which will allow drainage. Make at least three days in advance and keep in refrigerator.

If using large curd cheese, drain excess moisture by putting in a sieve, covering with a plate, and compressing with a 4 to 5 pound weight. Suspend over a bowl to catch the moisture and refrigerate over night.

Put the cheese (whichever kind is being used) through a sieve, blender or food processor until smooth and set aside. Thoroughly cream the butter, egg yolks, and sugar. Add the cheese and remaining ingredients and mix well. In a saucepan bring almost to boiling point over low heat, stirring constantly. Remove from heat before it begins to boil. Then allow to cool, stirring frequently. Mixture will be quite thin.

Line the mold with 2 layers of moistened cheesecloth, leaving enough cloth at the top to form a flap. Fill mold with the cheese mixture and cover with the flap. Put a plate on top, compress with a weight as above and refrigerate. Remove carefully onto a platter.

Yield: 8 to 10 servings.

Paskha, which means "Easter," is a vital part of the refreshments served to visitors during the gay Easter holidays. In addition to Paskha, a complete Easter table must have Kulich (page 33), Kooriza Zaleevnoie (page 15), colored Easter eggs, cold baked ham, various Zakooski (as Selyodka, page 42) and of course, a steaming samovar.

Piroznoie s Malinoii i Sbitimii Slivkamii

PASTRY with STRAWBERRY JAM and WHIPPED CREAM

Pastry:
- 2 cups flour
- ⅓ tsp. salt
- 1 cup shortening
- 5 to 6 tbsp. water

Filling:
- 1 cup strawberry jam
- 1 cup whipping cream, whipped

Cut shortening into flour and salt; add enough water to hold pastry together and mix lightly. On a floured board, form into four balls. Roll out each ball into an 8 inch round. Transfer onto a baking sheet. Prick with a fork and bake in a hot oven (425°F) for 12 to 15 minutes or until light brown.

Place a round of pastry on a large plate, spread with jam, top with whipped cream. The other rounds are laid on top of the first, each with its quota of jam and cream, the topmost layer being given an especially generous layer of whipped cream.

Yield: 8 servings.

In many a well-ordered Russian household, the puff paste Piroznoie rounds are kept on hand in an air-tight can, ready for an emergency "guest dessert."

Apelsinovii Pooding

RICE-ORANGE PUDDING

½ cup uncooked rice   ¼ tsp. salt
⅓ cup sugar   1 cup water

Combine the above ingredients in a saucepan, cover, bring to a boil, reduce heat and simmer until water is absorbed and rice is tender.

2 large juicy oranges   3 cloves
⅓ cup sugar   ⅔ cup boiling water

Peel the two oranges saving the rind from one orange. Remove the membrane from the orange sections and set them aside.

Chop the rind that has been saved and put it into a kettle with the remaining ingredients. Boil over medium heat for 5 minutes.

Shape the hot rice into a mound on a platter. Arrange orange sections on rice and pour the syrup over. Serve either hot or cold.

Yield: 4 servings.

Kulich
Easter Bread

BREADS
and
SMALL PASTRIES

Kulich

EASTER BREAD

2½ cups milk	1 tsp. vanilla or lemon extract
⅓ cup butter	or 3 drops oil of roses
¾ cup sugar	1 cup raisins
½ tsp. salt	1 cup candied fruit
1 package dry yeast	1 cup citron
or 1 yeast cake	1½ cups chopped almonds
8 cups flour	2 cups powdered sugar
3 egg yolks, beaten	1 tsp. vanilla
2 whole eggs, beaten	milk or cream

Warm the milk and add butter to melt it. Add the sugar and salt and cool until tepid. Add yeast and allow to dissolve. Slowly stir in 4 cups flour. Put in warm place, raise until double in bulk. Then add the beaten egg yolks, eggs and preferred flavoring. Mix the raisins, candied fruit, citron and almonds with the remaining flour and add to dough. Knead thoroughly and raise to double bulk.

When raised, shape to fit well greased cans (1 or 2 pound coffee cans are a good size). Fill cans two-thirds full and allow to rise in a warm place until dough is over rim of can. Bake in a moderate oven (350°F) for 45 to 60 minutes depending on size of loaf.

When baked, remove from container and allow to cool a little. While still warm, cover top with icing made from powdered sugar, vanilla and sufficient milk or cream to make it thin enough to run down the sides of the loaf. Decorate with small colored candies.

Yield: 3 to 4 loaves.

During the last week of Lent, the Russian housewife devotes great care to the making of her Kulich, for on its quality depends her rating as a cook. It is not eaten until after the Easter midnight service, and during the three days of open house after Easter there is always a decorated Kulich on the dining table.

Pletjonaja Boolka

BRAIDED ROLL

1 package dry yeast or 1 yeast cake	2 eggs, well beaten
	3¾ cups flour
1 cup milk, warmed	Topping:
¼ cup melted butter	1 egg yolk
½ cup sugar	1 tsp. melted butter
grated rind of 1 lemon	1 tbsp. sugar
½ tsp. almond extract	1 tsp. cinnamon

Soften yeast in warm milk. Add the one-fourth cup butter, one-half cup sugar, lemon rind, almond extract and eggs. Then stir in sifted flour, slowly. Knead well. Allow to rise until double in bulk; knead again. Roll out, cut in three long strips, and braid strips. Put onto greased pan; raise to double bulk. Moisten top with egg yolk mixed with butter and sprinkle with sugar and cinnamon. Cover loosely with foil and bake in a moderate oven (350°F) for 25 to 30 minutes.

Yield: 1 loaf.

Well known in nearly all countries except the U. S., the braided roll has much to recommend it. Having more character than bread, it provides a pleasant change from bread at any meal, especially with coffee. Serve it cold or hot (heat quickly in a hot oven), slice and toast it, or break it like French bread.

Vatrooshki

COTTAGE CHEESE TARTS

Puff paste:
- 1 cup flour
- ⅓ cup shortening
- ¼ tsp salt
- water

Filling:
- 1 cup cottage cheese
- 2 tbsp. sugar
- 1 beaten egg

Puff paste: Using only enough water to bind, make a pastry of the flour, shortening and salt. Roll out to an eighth inch thick and cut into 3 inch rounds. Pinch up the edges of the pastry making a shallow bowl of each and set on a cookie sheet.

Filling: Mix the cottage cheese, sugar and beaten egg. Put a heaping teaspoon of this mixture in the center of each round of pastry. Bake in a hot oven (450°F) 10 to 15 minutes or until the tarts are golden and will move easily on the pan. Serve with fruit salads or with coffee or tea.

Yield: About 30 tarts.

Suharji

CRACKNELS

1 package dry yeast	½ tsp. salt
or 1 yeast cake	2 cups flour
1 cup warm water	2 tbsp. poppyseed

Soften yeast in water. Add salt, flour and poppyseed, adding more flour if dough is not stiff enough to knead well. After thorough kneading, raise in a warm place to double bulk. Knead again, again raise double. Roll out very thin and cut into varied shapes having an area of about 2 square inches. Drop a few at a time into boiling water. As soon as they float, remove with a slotted spoon. Place on a cookie sheet and sprinkle lightly with salt. Bake in a moderate oven (350°F) until they turn golden. Dry thoroughly in a slow oven (200°F).

Yield: About 12 dozen.

These Cracknels go very well with appetizers much like the Zakooska Selyodka on page 42. Also, being so easily digested, they are excellent for children's tea parties.

Piroshki

CARROT-EGG TURNOVER

Puff paste:
- 1½ cups flour
- ⅓ tsp. salt
- ½ cup shortening
- water

Filling:
- 1 cup sliced carrot, cooked
- 2 eggs, hard boiled
- salt and pepper to taste

Puff paste: Sift flour and salt and cut in shortening with pastry cutter or two knives until the shortening is about the size of small peas. Add only enough water to hold pastry together; mix lightly; transfer to a floured board. Roll out, then fold in half and roll out four times, the last time to an eighth inch thickness. Cut into rounds with a 3 inch biscuit cutter.

Filling: Chop fine the carrots and eggs; season to taste and mix well without mashing.

On one half of each pastry round place a rounded teaspoon of filling. Moisten edges of round with water and fold over. With a fork press the edges together carefully and prick the top of each pastry. Bake in a hot oven (400° F) about 15 minutes or until golden brown.

Serve with clear soups or salads or as an appetizer. Unbaked Piroshki may be frozen by placing in a single layer on a cookie sheet.

Yield: About 3 dozen.

Replica of Russian Blockhouse
Sitka, Alaska

MISCELLANEOUS

Russkii Chai

RUSSIAN TEA

1 heaping tbsp. black tea
pinch of cloves
6 cups freshly boiled water
4 tsp. rum (optional)

Put tea and cloves into a small teapot which has been pre-heated. Add 1 cup water and let stand for 5 minutes. Pour a little into each glass, according to the strength desired and fill glass with additional boiling water. Add 1 tsp. rum to each glass if desired.

Yield: 4 servings.

Russian style tea should always be served in glasses, not cups, so that its lovely color may be enjoyed, as well as its aroma and flavor. Adding the rum makes it real Russian tea.

Zakooska Selyodka

SALT HERRING APPETIZER

2 salt herring (see below) 2 tbsp. chopped sweet pickle
3 tbsp. mayonnaise 1 hard boiled egg, chopped

Soak the herring for 24 hours, changing the water at least six times. Split fish down the back, remove from bone and pull off skin. Lay half herring on board and cut across into small sections (quarter inch or smaller), being careful to preserve shape of fish. Slide broad knife under the sectioned half fish and lift it carefully onto a platter. Cover with a dressing made of mayonnaise, egg and pickle.

Cut other half, lay it over first half, and cover with dressing. Lay second herring, prepared in the same way, beside the first.

Yield: Four to six servings, depending on size of herring.

Served with beer, wine or cocktails, Zakooska Selyodka makes an excellent appetizer. It is always part of the bountiful zakooska (hors d'oeuvres) that precedes Russian meals.

Salt herring may usually be purchased in specialty or Scandinavian food stores. Fresh herring may be salted as follows:

5 pounds herring 2 pounds rock salt

Clean herring by cutting through spine below gills and removing head, gills and gut in a single piece. Wash well in salt brine. Drain for about 10 minutes. Put a thin layer of salt in the bottom of a crock or bowl which has a tight fitting lid and straight sides. Then place a layer of herring, backs down. Scatter salt on top so that the layer is just covered. The next layer is packed at right angles to the preceding one. The top layer is packed with backs up and salted more generously. Close container tightly and store in a cool, dark place. As the salt dissolves add more until it is no longer absorbed indicating that a 100 percent solution has been attained. The herring are then ready for use.

Garchichij Sous

MUSTARD SAUCE

1 tbsp. dry mustard	½ cup vinegar
2 tbsp. sugar	1 tbsp. capers
3 egg yolks	1 tbsp. chopped green
2 tbsp. olive or other salad oil	olives

Mix mustard with sugar. In top of double boiler, beat egg yolks. Add mustard and sugar mixture, then slowly beat in the oil and vinegar. Cook over moderate heat in double boiler and continue to beat until thick. Add capers and olives.

Yield: 1 cup.

This sauce is delicious with meats, hot or cold, and is particularly recommended for Kooriza Zaleevnoie (page 15).

Notes